U.S. Department of Justice
Office of Justice Programs
National Institute of Justice

I0476620

The Threat of Russian Organized Crime

James O. Finckenauer and Yuri A. Voronin

Issues in
International Crime

U.S. Department of Justice
Office of Justice Programs
810 Seventh Street N.W.
Washington, DC 20531

John Ashcroft
Attorney General

Office of Justice Programs
World Wide Web Site
http://www.ojp.usdoj.gov

National Institute of Justice
World Wide Web Site
http://www.ojp.usdoj.gov/nij

The Threat of Russian Organized Crime

James O. Finckenauer and Yuri A. Voronin

June 2001
NCJ 187085

Issues in International Crime

National Institute of Justice

James O. Finckenauer is director of the International Center of the National Institute of Justice, which is the research arm of the U.S. Department of Justice. He is on leave from the Rutgers University School of Criminal Justice, where he is a professor of criminal justice. Professor Finckenauer is the author or coauthor of six books as well as numerous articles and reports. His latest books are *Russian Mafia in America* (Northeastern University Press, 1998) and *Scared Straight and the Panacea Phenomenon Revisited* (Waveland Press, 1999).

Yuri A. Voronin served as a visiting international fellow with the National Institute of Justice from March 1, 1999, to March 1, 2000. At the time of his fellowship, he was both a full professor at the Urals State Law Academy and director of the Organized Crime Study Center at the Urals State Law Academy.

Portions of this report were prepared for the National Institute of Justice, U.S. Department of Justice, under grant number 1999–IJ–CX–0014 to Yuri A. Voronin with funds transferred from the U.S. Department of State. Points of view or opinions stated in this document are those of the authors and do not necessarily represent the official position or policies of the U.S. Department of Justice.

The National Institute of Justice is a component of the Office of Justice Programs, which also includes the Bureau of Justice Assistance, the Bureau of Justice Statistics, the Office of Juvenile Justice and Delinquency Prevention, and the Office for Victims of Crime.

CONTENTS

INTRODUCTION

A long smear of blood on the road marks the place where two masked men shot dead one of Russia's most prominent industrialists . . . outside his house in the city of Yekaterinburg in the Ural Mountains. Oleg Belonenko, 51, managing director of Uralmash, the largest industrial company in Russia, had just got in this grey Volga car to go to work when two men in track-suits opened fire with pistols, hitting him in the head and his driver in the stomach. Both men died in hospital. Mr. Belonenko's murder . . . once again shows the power and ruthlessness of criminal gangs who control large sections of Russia's economy.[1]

In the decade since the collapse of the Soviet Union, the world has become the target of a new global crime threat from criminal organizations and criminal activities that have poured forth over the borders of Russia and other former Soviet republics such as Ukraine. The nature and variety of the crimes being committed seems unlimited—drugs, arms trafficking, stolen automobiles, trafficking in women and children, and money laundering are among the most prevalent. The spillover is particularly troubling to Europe (and especially Eastern Europe) because of its geographical proximity to Russia, and to Israel, because of its large numbers of Russian immigrants. But no area of the world seems immune to this menace, especially not the United States. America is the land of opportunity for unloading criminal goods and laundering dirty money. For that reason—and because, unfortunately, much of the examination of Russian organized crime (the so-called "Russian Mafia") to date has been rather hyperbolic and sketchy—we believe it is important to step back and take an objective look at this growing phenomenon. Just what is this Russian Mafia? What does it look like? Where does it come from? What does it do? And how does it do it? We hope that through addressing these questions we can provide a context for assessing how much of a threat Russian crime might be to the United States—directly or indirectly—and how concerned we should be.

Let us begin by providing some context for our discussion. First, the reader should know that defining organized crime is a matter of some dispute among scholars and law enforcement specialists. That disagreement is heightened when the subject, as in this case, becomes *transnational* organized crime. We will not, however, venture into this controversy here. Instead, we will simply provide our own working definition of organized crime:

Organized crime is crime committed by criminal organizations whose existence has continuity over time and across crimes, and that use systematic violence and corruption to facilitate their criminal activities. These criminal organizations have varying capacities to inflict economic, physical, psychological, and societal harm. The greater their capacity to harm, the greater the danger they pose to society.

As in the United States, there is no universally accepted definition of organized crime in Russia, in major part because Russian law (like U.S. law) provides no legal definition of organized crime. Analysis of criminological sources, however, enables one to identify some of its basic characteristics.[2] These include organizational features that make Russian organized crime unique in the degree to which it is embedded in the post-Soviet political system. At the same time, however, it has certain features in common with such other well-known varieties of organized crime as the Italian Mafia. The latter has a complicated history that includes both cooperation and conflict with the Italian state. Much more than was ever the case with the Italian Mafia, however, Russian organized crime is uniquely a descendant of the Soviet state.

Russian organized crime has come to plague many areas of the globe since the demise of the Soviet Union just more than a decade ago. The transnational character of Russian organized crime, when coupled with its high degree of sophistication and ruthlessness, has attracted the world's attention and concern to what has become known as a global Russian Mafia. Along with this concern, however, has come a fair amount of misunderstanding and stereotyping with respect to Russian organized crime. It is this combination that has stimulated our work on this report.

We want to try to clear up some of the misunderstanding and misinformation and also to try to ensure that where there is concern, it is well-founded. To do so, we will trace some of the contextual features—historical, political and economic—of Russian organized crime. We will look briefly at moves by the Russian government since 1991 to cope with its crime problem. Then we will present a case study of organized crime in the Urals region of Russia. It was there that the killings described in our opening vignette occurred. As with any case study, our purpose in focusing on the Urals is to capture and examine in microcosm what has otherwise been explored mostly in macrocosm and purely descriptive forms. We will conclude with a brief discussion of the real and potential impacts of Russian organized crime on the United States.

HISTORICAL, POLITICAL, AND ECONOMIC ASPECTS

Organized crime is a historical phenomenon that has existed for hundreds, and in some cases, for thousands of years in many different societies. But interestingly, unlike common crime, true organized crime as we define it is not present everywhere. Certain characteristics seem to differentiate countries burdened by organized crime from those that are not. Some of these characteristics appear simply to be coexisting conditions, whereas others are facilitators, and yet still others could actually qualify as causes of organized crime.

The general level of crime in a country is an apparent primary condition for organized crime. High-crime countries are more likely than low-crime countries to have organized crime. This is because organized crime and common crime are influenced by many of the same factors. Crime is related to the degree of urbanization and industrialization and to social disorganization—factors that produce criminal opportunities and thus more crime. Organized crime is especially likely to be more prevalent in cities and countries with advanced levels of economic development, the history of the Mafia in rural Sicily to the contrary notwithstanding. Economic development, industrialization, and urbanization both stimulate and facilitate demand for goods and services. These include goods and services that are illegal (such as drugs), regulated (such as cigarettes or guns), or simply in short supply. When there is a plentiful supply of a legal, unregulated product, there is no incentive for organized crime to become a supplier. When we have the opposite condition, however, then we typically see organized crime rising to fulfill the unmet demand. This demand may be for drugs, firearms, or sex workers, or it may be for a service such as protection or resolving disputes when there is no acceptable legal means of doing so.

The nature of the criminal opportunities available in a particular place also influences the presence of organized crime. The extent to which particular criminal opportunities can best be exploited or, perhaps, can only be exploited by criminal organizations also helps explain the presence or absence of organized crime. Some crimes can be committed quite easily by criminals acting alone or in an unorganized manner, but others cannot. The latter is especially true of crimes that are committed across national borders.

With respect to organized crime, certain geographical or infrastructure characteristics, such as the presence of seaports, international airports, strategic border locations, rich natural resources, and so on, provide special criminal opportunities that can best be exploited by criminals who are organized. More so than common crime, organized crime is fed by the presence of ethnic minorities who furnish a ready supply of both victims and the offenders to victimize them. Organized crime also thrives in environments characterized by a relatively high tolerance of deviance and a romanticization of crime figures, especially where government and law enforcement are weak or corrupt (the history of the Sicilian Mafia illustrates this).

We are not suggesting that any of these factors are causes of organized crime but, rather, that they create a favorable climate for its growth. The fundamental causes of organized crime are actually quite simple—greed and demand. The greed for money and power on the part of some is often (although not always) met by the demand of others for goods and services that are illegal or unavailable.

Russia is one of those unfortunate countries that has the receptive environment in which organized crime thrives. Organized crime is deeply rooted in the 400-year history of Russia's peculiar administrative bureaucracy, but it was especially shaped into its current form during the seven decades of Soviet hegemony that ended in 1991. This ancestry helps to explain the pervasiveness of organized crime in today's Russia and its close merger with the political system. Organized crime in Russia is an institutionalized part of the political and economic environment. It cannot, therefore, be fully understood without first understanding its place in the context of the Russian political and economic system.

Unlike Colombian, Italian, Mexican, or other well-known forms of organized crime, Soviet organized crime was not primarily based on ethnic or family structures. To help understand the difference, we can look to the history of organized crime in the United States for a contrasting portrait. As a number of scholars have pointed out,[3] organized crime provided a "crooked ladder of upward mobility" for some immigrants to the United States. Certain immigrants—sharing a common ethnicity, culture, and language, and, being on the bottom rung of the socioeconomic ladder, either having legitimate opportunities for advancement closed to them or rejecting the opportunities that were available—have turned to crime, and specifically organized crime, to get ahead. This crooked ladder for ethnic immigrants was not the driving force behind organized crime in the U.S.S.R. Instead, the Soviet criminal world—except in the Caucasus (e.g., Armenia, Chechnya, Georgia) and Central Asia (e.g., Uzbekistan)—was built around a vertical dependency of individuals whose coalescence into criminal groups was driven solely by their mutual participation in criminal activities. The connection among these professional criminals, in other words, was economic, rather than ethnic or familial.

4

Because organized crime is made up of criminals who conspire to carry out illegal acts, a degree of trust is necessary among those criminals. Coconspirators must be able to trust that their collaborators will not talk to the police or to anyone who might talk to the police, and that they will not cheat them out of their money. A shared ethnicity, with its common language, background, and culture, has historically been a foundation for trust among organized crime figures.

Yet ethnicity did not play the significant role in Soviet organized crime that it played in the United States. Instead, the Soviet prison system, in many ways, fulfilled functions that were satisfied by shared ethnicity in the United States. In the Soviet Union, a professional criminal class developed in Soviet prisons during the Stalinist period that began in 1924—the era of the gulag. These criminals adopted behaviors, rules, values, and sanctions that bound them together in what was called the thieves' world, led by the elite "vory v zakone," criminals who lived according to the "thieves' law."[4] This thieves' world, and particularly the vory, created and maintained the bonds and climate of trust necessary for carrying out organized crime.

Organized crime in the Soviet era consisted of illegal enterprises with both legal and black-market connections that were based on the misuse of state property and funds. It is most important to recognize that the blurring of the distinction between the licit and the illicit is also a trademark of post-Soviet organized crime that shows its ancestry with the old Soviet state and its command-economy system. This, in turn, has direct political implications. The historical symbiosis with the state makes Russian organized crime virtually an inalienable part of the state. As this has continued into the present, some would say it has become an engine of the state that works at all levels of the Russian government.

Contemporary Russian organized crime grew out of the Soviet "nomenklatura" system (the government's organizational structure and high-level officials) in which some individual "apparatchiks" (government bureaucrats) developed mutually beneficial personal relationships with the thieves' world. The top of the pyramid of organized crime during the Soviet period was made up of the Communist Party and state officials who abused their positions of power and authority. Economic activities ranged across a spectrum of markets—white, gray, black, and criminal. These markets were roughly defined by whether the goods and services being provided were legal, legal but regulated, or illegal, and by whether the system for providing them was likewise legal, legal but regulated, or illegal. The criminals operated on the illegal end of this spectrum. Tribute gained from black markets and criminal activities was passed up a three-tiered pyramid to the nomenklatura, and the nomenklatura itself (some 1.5 million people) had a vast internal system of rewards and punishments. The giant state apparatus thus not only allowed criminal activity, but encouraged, facilitated, and protected it, because the apparatus itself benefited from crime.

These sorts of relationships provided the original nexus between organized crime and the government. From these beginnings, organized crime in Russia evolved to its present ambiguous position of being both in direct collaboration with the state and, at the same time, in conflict with it.

Specialists in Russian organized crime date the appearance of the first organized criminal groups in the former Soviet Union to the end of the 1960s.[5] It was then that the three-tiered edifice known collectively as the Russian Mafia began to take shape. As indicated, the top level of this structure was occupied by high-level government and party bureaucrats. The second level consisted of underground or shadow economy participants who exploited their jobs or connections with the enterprises of the state-command economy for illicit gain. The shadow economy produced goods and services "off the books," that is, outside the state-mandated production quotas, and the payment for these goods and services went into the pockets of these occupants of the second tier. On the bottom level were the professional criminals who ran the various illegal activities such as drugs, gambling, prostitution, extortion, and so on.

Before the 1960s, the three levels of organized crime existed separately, and their paths rarely crossed. This changed when the traditional criminal world began to become intertwined with the economic or white-collar criminals of the shadow economy and with the party bureaucracy. According to Stephen Handelman's account of the rise of the "comrade criminals" in Russia, "the black marketeers of the 1960s and 1970s crossed the line dividing the underworld and the state. They operated in easy and mutually profitable cooperation with Soviet bureaucrats."[6] This intertwining reflected the pervasive nature of corruption during the "period of stagnation" under Soviet leader Leonid Brezhnev (1964–82). Government and party officials left no stones unturned in seeking opportunities to line their pockets. One such opportunity was extorting money from the criminal world and the shadow economy in exchange for protecting their illegal operations. This complicated chain of organized crime worked its way from the bottom to the top of Soviet society. It ultimately included state finances, industry, trade, and the system of public services.[7]

During the presidency of Mikhail Gorbachev (1985–91), private enterprise, in the form of cooperatives, was encouraged in the U.S.S.R. This was a dramatic shift from what had been the prevailing Soviet socialist model of the economy, in which most private enterprise was outlawed. Unfortunately, the people best positioned to take advantage of this new opportunity were the criminals, the underground producers, and the bureaucrats who collaborated with them. These collaborators knew how to make money and had all the necessary connections to conduct business successfully, and the new policy enabled them to start to operate more openly. Toward the end of the Gorbachev period, when there were unmistakable signs that the Soviet Union was about to implode, the insiders—high-level officials in the central and regional headquarters of the Communist Party—began quietly to siphon off Party funds into banks, trading companies, and export-import firms, to position themselves to take advantage of what was expected to be a new economic era.[8] This was a classic case of trading political advantage for economic advantage. By the late 1980s, corruption had reached such high levels that it was, for example, possible for any criminal to bribe his way out of any lawbreaking problem. The result of this combination of the "theft of the state" and the corruption was a massive increase in lawlessness and the rise of a new type of organized crime that has since permeated nearly every level of society in the former Soviet Union.

POLITICAL AND ECONOMIC LINKAGES

The privatization of state property that began in Russia in 1992—when public property began to be sold to private investors—both expanded and solidified the complex relationship that had developed between the state and organized crime. Because of its connections to officialdom and to the shadow economy, organized crime took part in what has become the enormously lucrative scheme of privatization. As a result, the assets controlled by organized crime give it enormous economic power, and hence political power as well. These assets enable criminal organizations (in various guises) to deal directly with the state—on behalf of their own economic interests—from a position of parity. Organized crime has also attempted to assume certain governmental functions, such as dividing territories among competing economic actors and regulating business markets.[9] It seeks to control business-market entry, to impose taxes (protection fees), to set up tariffs, and—as is characteristic of organized crime in the United States—to enforce all this through direct violence or other forms of coercion. It is the latter activities that have laid the groundwork for direct conflict with the state, because only the state can legitimately use violence. This series of developments is as much political and economic as it is criminological, and it is unlike anything we have ever seen in the United States.

Organized crime in Russia uses legal businesses as fronts for illegal activities and for setting up illegal product lines.[10] It creates "political clans" to exercise political power and seeks to create and regulate markets to exercise economic power. The following are some specific characteristics of Russian organized crime in the post-Soviet era:

■ Russian criminals make extensive use of the state governmental apparatus to protect and promote their criminal activities. For example, most businesses in Russia—legal, quasi-legal, and illegal—must operate with the protection of a "krysha" (roof). The protection is often provided by police or security officials employed outside their "official" capacities for this purpose. In other cases, officials are "silent partners" in criminal enterprises that they, in turn, protect.

■ The criminalization of the privatization process has resulted in the massive use of state funds and property for criminal gain. Valuable properties are purchased through insider deals for much less than their true value and then resold for lucrative profits.

■ Criminals have been able to directly influence the state's domestic and foreign policy to promote the interests of organized crime, either by attaining public office themselves or by buying public officials.

Beyond these particular features, organized crime in Russia shares other characteristics that are common to some other forms of organized crime elsewhere in the world:

■ Systematic use of violence, including both the threat and the use of force.

■ Hierarchical structure.

■ Limited or exclusive membership.

■ Specialization in types of crime and a division of labor.

■ Military-style discipline, with strict rules and regulations for the organization as a whole.

■ Possession of high-tech equipment, including military weapons.[11]

The flexibility and dynamism of the new organized crime give it a distinct advantage in the competition for political and economic control with the rigidly bureaucratic state institutions in Russia's cities and regions. Through networks of financial-industrial groups or holding companies, central and regional organized crime groups penetrate into each other's territory, where they struggle for political and economic spheres of influence. The expansion of organized crime in Moscow, for example, has occurred through buying real estate, and through gaining controlling shares of banks and other enterprises. These crime groups, in turn, are buying up controlling shares in various regional banks and enterprises on a broader regional level outside of Moscow.[12]

Russian organized crime operates successfully throughout the former Soviet Union, engaging in such activities as money laundering, drug trafficking, and the illegal sale of weapons. The bonds between the criminal organizations of Russia and those of the other Newly Independent States (NIS) can be easily traced back to their old Soviet nomenklatura connections. Many of the players are the same; only the name of the game is different. The new game is widely known as "nomenklatura capitalism."[13] Unfortunately, this characterization does not capture the true criminal nature of the post-Soviet economy. The combination of political and economic resources, lack of accountability, and vast territorial presence facilitates the continued expansion of Russian organized crime and compels us to take its political and global implications most seriously.

THE LEGAL AND LAW ENFORCEMENT CONTEXT

Since 1991, Russian law and the criminal justice system have gone through significant changes. Among the changes relevant to organized crime are increased sanctions for crimes committed by groups (and especially for their leaders) and new provisions on extortion.[14] As with other legal changes, however, there has been a continuing problem of weak law enforcement and an overall weakness of governmental authority. As a result, the law on the books is not the law in practice.

The laws on corruption and organized crime remain only drafts as of this writing.[15] Neither draft holds much promise of making substantive changes to the Russian Criminal Code. The draft law on corruption follows a Presidential decree (by President Yeltsin) in laying out a spectrum of responses to breaches of the rules. These responses range from disciplining guilty employees to firing them and banning them from further employment in government to criminal prosecution (on the basis of charges already provided for in the existing Criminal Code). The main thrust of the draft law on corruption lies not in the response to instances of corruption that are exposed but in measures designed to increase the detection of wrongdoing. The draft versions of the law include the mandatory disclosure of the ownership of real estate, other property, and financial assets in large amounts, including the numbers of bank accounts. Critics of the law condemn these disclosure rules as violations of privacy rights.

The draft law on organized crime deals mainly with law enforcement and has been strongly criticized for violating individual rights. Whether Russian legislators will ultimately be satisfied with either of these drafts remains to be seen. In the meantime, inconsistencies between the 1996 Criminal Code and a heavily amended criminal procedure code from the Soviet era have impeded the effective prosecution of crimes.

What do these legal developments mean for organized crime and for the efforts of authorities to confront it? For one thing, the current gaps in the legal system have facilitated illegal activities pursued by criminal organizations. In addition, inadequate law enforcement and a lack of public faith in the law and legal institutions have encouraged illegal activity and its connections to corrupt officials. To combat organized crime and corruption, or at least to appear to combat it, the Russian government has acted in ways that have actually worked against legal and judicial reform, for example, carrying out dubious raids on media outlets that have been critical of the government. Such raids have been a highly visible and controversial tool of the Putin regime.

No serious effort has been made within the Russian government to define "organized crime" in legal terms as the broad and complex phenomenon that it is. The Russian government has yet to formulate a coherent overall strategy for fighting crime in general. It has also failed to address challenges presented to law enforcement efforts by organized crime in particular. Official corruption remains rampant. There is no witness protection program. While the legal apparatus and law enforcement resources for fighting organized crime remain undeveloped and inadequate, criminal organizations unfortunately flourish. Let us turn in the next section to a specific case in point: the story of organized crime in the Russian Urals.

THE DEVELOPMENT OF ORGANIZED CRIME IN THE URALS

Some 900 miles east of Moscow, in Russia's Ural Mountains, lies the city of Yekaterinburg. Known in Soviet days as Sverdlovsk, Yekaterinburg is the largest industrial center in Russia, with a population of 1.5 million people. It has an extensive military-industrial complex, built to take advantage of the region's mineral wealth and its status as a transportation hub. The Ural Mountains mark the boundary that divides European and Asian Russia. This is an area known for its historical significance, as well as its vast repository of rich natural resources. Former Russian President Boris Yeltsin was born there and ruled for many years as the governor of the Sverdlovsk region, which includes Yekaterinburg. It was also here that, in 1918, the last Russian czar, Nicholas II, and his family were shot to death by the Bolsheviks in the name of the Great October Socialist Revolution.

Since the end of the Soviet Union in 1991, Yekaterinburg has been in the forefront of those Russian cities and territories struggling to loosen Moscow's grip on their affairs. Regrettably, it has acquired another less laudatory distinction as well—that of being the "gangster capital of Russia." Today, Yekaterinburg is one of Russia's most violent cities, with shootouts and contract killings reminiscent of gangland Chicago in the 1920s. The Sverdlovsk region, for instance, experienced a 68 percent increase in serious crimes from 1998 to 1999. How and why this explosion of crime, and in particular organized crime, has occurred—and its global implications—are the subject of this case study.[16]

The history and nature of crime in the Urals is very much linked to the history of industrial development in the former Soviet Union. It was in this region that major industrial sites were built in the beginning of the U.S.S.R.'s economic boom of the 1930s. The early work force that manned this boom was made up not only of ordinary workers but also of large numbers of political prisoners and common criminals who were confined in the prison camps—nerve endings in Stalin's vast gulag—that dotted the area. There are families in Yekaterinburg today in which almost all the family members going back for three or four generations have been prisoners. Their communities often treat residents who have never been imprisoned as outsiders because they are not "normal." As a result, crime in Yekaterinburg is family based and intergenerational to an extent unprecedented in any other region of the country. Generations of young persons, especially those without formal education, have been practically limited to joining criminal organizations as their means of livelihood. Yet even for others, working in state-run enterprises during the Soviet era was never particularly attractive to the youth of the region. Crime and its practitioners, on the other hand, were seen as less hypocritical, and in many ways more honest, than working with corrupt bureaucrats and officials. On top of that, there was the additional (and universal) attraction of the romantic aura surrounding crime.

By the late 1980s, two of the forerunners of today's organized crime were actively operating in the Urals region. The first we will call "white collar" criminals. Its practitioners were made up of a group of shadowy operatives known as "tsekhoviks," many of them clandestine millionaires, who had long been plundering state-owned enterprises and property. Founders of an underground economy known as the shadow economy, they were more akin to businessmen (albeit shady businessmen) than

11

to professional crooks. As a consequence, they did not possess the traditions or employ the methods of professional criminals, and in particular, they did not use violence in their criminal pursuits. The criminal opportunities to be exploited were so great that the tsekhoviks did not need to compete with one another but simply focused their efforts on maximizing their gains from underground and illegal production.

Cooperation between white-collar operatives in the shadow economy, those who operated in the black market (dealing in goods that were either illegal or in short supply), and ordinary criminals dates back to the 1960s, as we indicated earlier. But it was in the 1980s, during the Brezhnev and immediate post-Brezhnev era (Leonid Brezhnev was Soviet leader for nearly two decades), that this cooperation flourished. For example, in the mid-1980s, the Uralmash criminal group (Uralmash, located in Yekaterinburg, is Russia's largest heavy mechanical engineering plant) was active in the black market. At that time, the two brothers who were the leaders of the Uralmash group supervised contraband operations that were based upon receiving finished goods from the management of the Uralmash plant.[17] In exchange, the brothers financed lavish receptions for the factory managers. The latter was especially welcome because Moscow had sharply reduced Uralmash's budget and the plant was facing serious financial difficulties.

For strategic reasons, even greater collaboration between tsekhoviks and "real" criminals began to occur in the late 1980s. One strategy was to find ways to invest and launder illegally earned money. To do so, the underground moneymakers began to reach certain arrangements with the leaders of criminal gangs in the region. Two of the most influential tsekhoviks in the area—the father and son Tarlanov—became more directly involved in crime through such arrangements. As a result, they became kingpins not only in the shadow economy but also in the greater world of crime in the Sverdlovsk region. These dual connections gave them brains and muscle and facilitated their success in the nonferrous metals market, and in energy transport in particular. The relationship of another tsekhovik—the economist Viktor Ternyak— with leaders of the same Uralmash criminal group likewise led to the establishment and prospering of a conglomerate of investment firms and companies. These include the European-Asian Company, which had great success in the rare metals (e.g., silver) market.

Along with these developments, the vory v zakone began to expand their reach and power in the Sverdlovsk region in the 1980s. Throughout the former Soviet Union, the vory had long been regarded as the elite of the criminal world. They were hard-core professional criminals spawned by the gulag prison camps. To contrast them with the white-collar shadow businessmen, these professional criminals became known in criminal slang as the "blues," a name that some believe derived from the blue color of the tattoos that were associated with the vory v zakone. The vory were adherents of the traditional criminal mores developed in the camps and followed a strict thieves' code.

In addition to their common criminal activities that included such staples as assault, robbery, and theft, the blues began to organize and impose their criminal ideologies (the traditions of the vory v zakone) on other criminals, including those who were not prisoners or ex-prisoners. They began to build larger and more powerful criminal networks (loose collections of criminals and criminal groups organized around certain leaders, criminal specialties or markets, and territories). These networks took on the role of arbiters in the criminal community.[18]

Ultimately, conflict between the white-collar and blue branches of this evolving underworld in Sverdlovsk was inevitable. The criminal orthodoxy of the blues was unreceptive to the new thinking represented by the distinctively economic criminals. As active penetration of the legal economy by aspiring criminal entrepreneurs began in earnest in the latter 1980s, the blues found themselves on the outside. The white-collar entrepreneurs, who were made up of persons who had left the shadow economy and in some cases gained respectable public images, began to employ some of the methods of the criminal world, including the use of violence to eliminate competitors and business associates. Yet the vory, as well as some other criminal leaders who did not necessarily share their prison camp traditions and ideology, remained a definite presence on the criminal scene. As the decade of the 1990s began, this latter conglomeration constituted the core of a powerful, influential, and extensive criminal network of blues in Yekaterinburg and throughout the Sverdlovsk region.

The new Russian organized crime

The initial opposition between these two branches of crime changed in a major way in the mid-1990s. This period was marked by the privatization of the state-command economy and the breakdown of the rigid economic and political structures of the old Soviet totalitarian regime. In addition, the loss of moral and legal underpinnings that has sorely plagued post-Soviet Russia was a significant contextual factor in the growth of crime. Strategic raw materials such as nonferrous and rare metals, jewels, timber, and various products of the military-industrial complex flowed out in great quantities from the Urals region to the West—most of it smuggled. This illegal export fueled the growth of white-collar crime and, in turn, generated a wave of general crime as well. The new criminal entrepreneurs who were fomenting and exploiting this massive export soon became the targets of the blues' interest. The latter, quite naturally, were not about to ignore the prosperity of their brethren in the shadow economy and began putting direct pressure on them. To protect their businesses and themselves from violence, the new economic criminals were forced to begin sharing their profits with the old criminal leaders of the blue branch.

The result of this forced marriage was a merging of general or more traditional organized crime and the new forms of economic organized crime. New types of criminal groups emerged and then joined into larger criminal networks. Organized crime in the region acquired fresh features that continue to the present. Among these new features is the fact that the leaders of different criminal groups started splitting Yekaterinburg into large territorial sectors defined by spheres of influence.

By 1990–91, the Uralmash criminal group had become a network occupying the preeminent position in the shadowy world of business and crime in the Sverdlovsk region. Their criminal activities were broad ranging, including everything from rackets to trading in rare metals. Particularly lucrative was their export trade in nonferrous metals and titanium. They continued to help the Uralmash industrial plant—which suffered severely from the loss of the state-guaranteed market for its products—by buying up its finished products for marketing. The diversified interests of the Uralmash group included the local soccer team, restaurants, automobile dealerships, hotels, and other commercial enterprises, including their own brokerage firm.

Today, the Uralmash criminal network personifies the new type of criminal organization that now dominates organized crime in Russia. They generally ignore the old thieves' code of the vory v zakone, but do employ strict discipline and subordination to their leadership. Instead of looking to the vory or other professional criminals for their membership, they recruit former athletes and police officers. Not surprisingly, open warfare has broken out between the old and new forms of organized crime, resulting in assassinations, kidnapings, torture, explosions, and street shootings in Yekaterinburg and other cities of the Urals. Similar violence has ensued from competition over control of the various strategic commercial enterprises of the Sverdlovsk region. The continuing crime war has resulted in the killings of many leaders, as well as of mid-level and rank-and-file members.

In addition to the original shadow-economy artists who were major participants in the Uralmash criminal network, a group based in the central district of Yekaterinburg emerged.[19] Preferring to avoid clashes with law enforcement authorities that might ensue from direct involvement in overt criminal activities, this central group has pursued global investment projects, the export of strategic raw materials, and illicit real-estate market operations, e.g., buying up real estate for money-laundering purposes. In addition, they control many commercial enterprises in the central districts of Yekaterinburg, including insurance companies, casinos, fashionable restaurants, and the street trade of the central marketplace. They control gambling through their "Globus" business club.[20] The central group is also associated with representatives of legal businesses, is co-owner of the Urals commodity and raw materials exchange, and contributes to a variety of charities.

The Uralmash network, despite being portrayed in the media as a respectable financial and industrial group, dominates the criminal world of the Sverdlovsk region. Among other activities, they settle disputes between subsidiary criminal groups. In addition to ignoring the thieves' code of the vory v zakone, they have even removed old vory from leadership positions in the criminal community. Unlike Moscow-based criminal organizations, Uralmash and, in particular, the central group, do not make payments to the blues' traditional central fund (the "obshchak"), a collection of money that is used as a kind of welfare fund for vory and their associates who are imprisoned, as well as for their families. The Uralmash network relies increasingly on muscle and less upon arbitration for settling disputes. In this, they are more like criminal organizations and networks in St. Petersburg than like those in Moscow. As a result, the thieves' code and ideology has diminished in importance in Yekaterinburg and St. Petersburg, where it has been pushed aside by young aggressive leaders who are focused on laundering their illegal income by investing in legal businesses.

Violence reaches new levels

Conflict and violence have marked the competition among various criminal groups and between the white collars and the blues, and this violence has been taken to new heights. In the fall of 1992, for example, the Uralmash criminal network, which was by far the strongest in the region, created a special team to handle the "physical elimination" of leaders of rival organized criminal groups. It recruited former special-forces training instructors and trainees from the military who were expert in elimination methods.[21]

This action was met in kind by the central network, which created its own "hit" team. Thus, two opposing assassination teams were formed within the same region and sphere of criminal activity.[22] This testifies to the extreme means to which the new Russian organized crime will resort in settling disputes. It also says something about the new sophistication in the use of violence. These were both highly professional operations that carried out assassination on order, with the protection of corrupted officials.[23]

The blues strike back

One reaction to the struggle between Uralmash and the central group was a coming together of the blues—the original criminal community including the vory v zakone. This coming together served three purposes: maintaining the authority of the vory in the prison system, strengthening the blues' resistance to control of the new forms of economic organized crime by the Uralmash and central groups, and adapting their own criminal endeavors to the evolving market and political conditions.

Leadership of the blues went to a group of vory who were regarded as smart enough and tough enough to take up the challenge to the old guard.[24] To meet this challenge successfully, they required the support of the underworld of blues elsewhere in the country, continued strength in the prisons to feed the ranks with new recruits, and connections with important officials. By the mid-1990s, previously isolated groups of professional criminals had been merged into a greater criminal network in Yekaterinburg. The key figures in this network were all vory.

Critical to the survival of the vory v zakone and other blues in Yekaterinburg was their ability to further their own economic interests, to invest the concentrated capital they controlled that was otherwise just sitting in the obshchak, and, in general, to increase their influence in the region. As witness to their success in accomplishing these ends, the blues today control a number of areas of economic activity (e.g., gas stations, some aspects of the oil business, timber, and nonferrous and precious metals). Despite their cooperative success, however, the battle over spheres of influence has not ended. Since 1995, a number of the leaders have either died or been killed. This random, personal-vendetta type of violence reflects a degree of instability in the larger criminal community and is evidence that no one criminal organization has been able to exert monopoly control over the various areas of criminal activity.

CONTEMPORARY ISSUES CONCERNING ORGANIZED CRIME IN THE URALS

Statistical data on organized crime groups and their members in Russia are subject to a number of reservations. These include questions about how the terms "organized crime" and "organized crime group" are defined and the bases for counting membership in such groups. Nevertheless, such data provide a snapshot of the law enforcement perspective on the magnitude of the problem. According to the Organized

Crime Section of the Russian Ministry of Internal Affairs, 124 organized criminal groups with 1,318 members operated in the Sverdlovsk region in 1998. By early 1999, the numbers had grown to 142 groups with 1,424 members. These numbers are considerably larger than those of just 5 years before. It is further estimated that 362 commercial businesses are under the control of organized crime.

The Urals, and the Sverdlovsk region in particular, have been hit harder by organized crime than any other area of the country. Its industrial potential, rich natural resources, and geographic location make for especially lucrative plundering. The merging of traditional crime and the new economic crime, money laundering, and the extensive use of firearms and explosives are especially characteristic of this region. The redistribution of property from the state to private hands under Russia's privatization initiative has been controlled in Sverdlovsk by criminal networks, at tremendous cost to the region's economic development. Similarly, the attempt to develop foreign markets for the region's industrial products has attracted criminal interests. As if matters were not bad enough, Moscow-based criminal organizations and other outside groups are competing for control with the home grown criminal networks. The methods used in this competition are the same as in the early 1990s: corruption, blackmail, threats, and hired assassins.

As the most criminal region of the country, the Urals has certain other distinctive features. For example, it has become known as a "bespredel" (without rules) zone, an area where the thieves' code has no power. The vory v zakone have less influence in the Urals than in any other region of Russia. This means the local criminal organizations, such as the Uralmash and central groups, do not bow to any nationwide criminal networks. At the same time, it means they do not gain the latter's support. This independence is contrary to the trend in other parts of the former Soviet Union, where there has been a consolidation of the strength of the vory. Independence results in greater conflict with criminal organizations from elsewhere in Russia or the former Soviet Union, but at the same time, it brings relative stability in the zones and spheres of influence among the Urals criminal groups themselves. The latter does not mean, as indicated earlier, that there are not continuing efforts to gain competitive advantage.

The underworld in Yekaterinburg is much better organized than it is in Moscow. The enormous sums of money going into the hands of criminal leaders have facilitated their purchase of state-of-the-art weapons, the recruitment of new members, and the bribery of officials, as well as the organization of detachments of trained killers drawn from the special forces of the Russian army. Internal organization has created sections devoted to counteracting the efforts of law enforcement, vertical

17

hierarchies of authority, and severe punishments for any who violate the rules. Because there is general agreement on the division of the spheres of influence, disputes can usually be settled without violence.

The availability of alternatives for dispute resolution does not mean, by any stretch of the imagination, that violence has disappeared. Physical elimination—assassination or killing—is still an important tool for doing business, but it is a tool that is only used when other means are deemed inappropriate or have been exhausted. This is unlike the situation in Moscow, for example, where physical elimination is often the only means for resolving conflicts between criminal organizations.

The criminal leaders of Yekaterinburg and the Sverdlovsk region are well connected with the city and regional governing authorities, and use their financial power both for bribery and to influence the outcomes of elections. The same is true in the commercial and banking sectors. Bribery, threats, blackmail, and violence are used to penetrate business management and assume control of commercial enterprises, or in some instances, to found their own enterprises with money from their criminal activities.

The three power centers of organized crime

The three most powerful criminal networks in Yekaterinburg today continue to be the Uralmash group, the central group, and the blues. The Uralmash group is the most dangerous of the three. They are well-organized both vertically (having a hierarchical command structure) and horizontally (across various criminal enterprises), with a clear delineation of functions. They are also especially well connected to the political authorities and to law enforcement. They control a number of government officials who use their positions on behalf of Uralmash. Their control of a law firm in the city, for instance, enables them to exert their influence directly on the police and the City Department of Internal Affairs.

It is estimated that the Uralmash group controls some 140 commercial enterprises, including a network of banking and lending institutions. They are heavily engaged in exporting raw materials, rare and precious metals, weapons, medicines, and, from time to time, radioactive materials. Their international connections extend to China, Cyprus, Germany, Poland, and the United States, among other countries.

The "central" criminal group has lost much of its leadership in recent years through arrest or assassination. At the same time, some new criminal alliances have been formed with veterans of the Soviet Union's disastrous military adventure in

Afghanistan. The latter are disgruntled soldiers who returned home from that lost war with few prospects, but trained and hardened by their experience in using weapons and in killing. They have been willing and able recruits for many criminal organizations across Russia.

The efforts of new figures to fill the central group's leadership vacuum have resulted in internal conflict and in increased potential for internecine violence and warfare. The group continues, however, to keep the focus of its criminal activity upon certain economic targets (e.g., international trading in nonferrous metals and other strategic resources, insurance, guaranteeing interbank loans, and the stock market). White-collar crimes and corruption remain their stock-in-trade. The central group is still well connected, both politically and with the new industrial and economic enterprises that dominate the region.

Although not as economically powerful and influential as its rivals, the blues' criminal network is the most numerous. This union of professional criminals continues the tradition of the obshchak—the monetary or welfare fund for prisoners and their families. Their financial base comes from payments by criminals and criminal groups into the obshchak—as a sort of "mob tax"—and from the extortion of money from businesses and commercial establishments. The blues have maintained regular contact with vory v zakone across Russia—in Moscow, Perm, Chelyabinsk, and Krasnodar. Sources report that six vory are active in the Sverdlovsk region today, with dominance being exerted by several former prison leaders from the Caucasus region. Relations among these leaders, however, remain ambiguous and complicated.

In Nizhni Tagil, another large industrial center in Sverdlovsk, the blues are the dominant criminal organization. There they are divided into brigades by geographical territory and criminal activity. They are well armed and well connected with criminal organizations in Central Asia, the Transcaucasus, and Turkey.

In sum, the criminal network known as the blues continues to have an influential presence in this region, but less so than in some other areas of the former Soviet Union. In keeping with the traditions of the vory v zakone, they render support to criminals who are imprisoned. They are independent in their criminal activity, but maintain "business relations" with criminal groups in Moscow, St. Petersburg, and certain cities in Siberia. They cultivate their immunity from law enforcement by maintaining corrupt relations with the police. They have not, however, penetrated the region's large industrial enterprises, as the Uralmash and central networks have.

Together, these three powerful criminal networks embrace the larger cities of the Sverdlovsk region like an octopus. In addition to controlling such traditional activities as rackets, prostitution, gambling, drugs, and arms trafficking, they have heavily infiltrated numerous business and commercial enterprises, and they are involved in both legal and illegal businesses abroad. To protect and facilitate all this activity, these criminal networks actively support political candidates and programs that are viewed to be working in their best interests. In some cases, they have formed their own political movements and parties. (See "Summary of the Criminal Activities of the Three Major Criminal Organizations in the Urals" on the next page.)

Organized crime in the economy

As the old Soviet state-command economy slowly evolves on its tortuous road to a "free market" system, organized crime has been quick to take advantage of this evolution. Throughout Russia, criminal organizations have moved into key industries, into the nascent money and banking sectors, and into the still-emerging stock market. Nowhere is this more apparent than in the Sverdlovsk region of the Urals. Through various forms of financial and securities fraud, illegal exports (including the export of capital), and other, more directly strong-arm tactics, the criminal networks of the Urals have effectively driven out, frightened off, or taken control of legitimate businesses and businessmen in the Sverdlovsk region. As a consequence, they now control, for example, the Lobvinsky Hydrolysis Plant—a highly profitable business that produces a variety of wood-based liquid products such as wood alcohol, but that is also used for the illegal but highly lucrative production of vodka. Likewise, the mob-controlled Kirovograd Copper Smelter had 777 kg of gold stolen by its management. Similar control is exercised over the Malyshev Mining Company that deals in precious stones, and over the Aluminum Production Plant.

The magnitude of this type of criminal activity in the region's economy is revealed in part by the increases in the number of "economic crimes committed by organized criminal groups" that have been investigated by law enforcement authorities. There were 203 such cases in 1996 and 480 in 1997; there were 284 in the first half of 1998 alone. The latter cases accounted for some 58 million rubles ($2 million) in lost sales and stolen raw materials and money.

One of the prominent characteristics of this economic organized crime is the amount of violence associated with it. Killings of businessmen, assaults, and other violent acts are so common that retaining some kind of security is a must for the survival of any business. According to investigative and trial data, nearly all the killings for hire in the region are connected to organized crime. A case in point is in the fuel and energy

> ## Summary of the Criminal Activities of the Three Major Criminal Organizations in the Urals
>
> *THE URALMASH CRIMINAL COMMUNITY*
> Occupies the preeminent position in the shadowy world of business and crime in the Sverdlovsk region. Typical activities include:
> - Rackets, kidnapings, and assassinations.
> - Corruption.
> - Illegal export trade in nonferrous metals and titanium.
> - Running the local soccer team, restaurants, automobile dealerships, hotels, and other commercial enterprises, including its own brokerage firm.
> - Money laundering.
> - Contributing to a charity.
> - Settling disputes between subsidiary criminal groups.
>
> *THE CENTRAL CRIMINAL GROUP*
> A group based in the central district of Yekaterinburg. It pursues:
> - Global investment projects.
> - The export of strategic raw materials.
> - Illicit real-estate market operations.
> - Commercial enterprises, including insurance companies, casinos, fashionable restaurants, and the street trade of the central marketplace.
> - Corruption.
> - Money laundering.
> - Extortion and gambling.
>
> In addition, it is co-owner of the Urals commodity and raw materials exchange and contributes to a wide variety of charities.
>
> *THE BLUES CRIMINAL COMMUNITY*
> Includes the vory v zakone. This coming together served three purposes:
> - Maintaining the authority of the vory in the prison system.
> - Strengthening the blues' resistance to control of the new forms of economic organized crime by the Uralmash and central groups.
> - Adapting their own criminal endeavors.
>
> The blues today control:
> - A number of areas of economic activity (e.g., gas stations, some aspects of the oil business, timber, and nonferrous and precious metals).
> - Corruption, blackmail, and hired assassins.
> - Extortion.
> - Drug and arms trafficking.

sector, where a number of small entrepreneurs have lost money and been forced to turn to such energy monopolists as Sverdlovenrego and Uraltransgazprom to bail them out. When these debts are not repaid, both creditors and debtors turn to mobsters—the former to enforce debt collection, and the latter to receive protection from their creditors. In a period of a week and a half in March and April 1998, three men in the oil business were shot in different cities in the Sverdlovsk region.

When otherwise legitimate businesses turn to organized crime to enforce debt collection, one often unexpected drawback is that they suffer from having "gotten into bed with the devil." Businessmen commonly employ for debt collection criminal groups that operate under the guise of security firms and are legally registered as such. The court system for arbitrating financial disputes is so inefficient and outmoded that procedures can last for months or even years. Thus it is easier, more efficient, and most important, faster, for businesses to turn to security firms controlled by organized crime than to rely upon the courts. In this way, Russian organized crime has taken on certain governmental functions, much as the Mafia did in Sicily.

Criminal organizations forcibly expand their partnerships with businesses that may have initially invited them in, to use them for money laundering. This money laundering is often carried out through directing or controlling the foreign economic activities of commercial enterprises. The criminal organizations use licenses, contracts, and overseas sales agreements to maintain accounts in foreign banks and thus evade taxation. It should be pointed out that high rates of taxation and tax evasion and blackmail, threats, violence, and corruption involving tax inspectors and the tax police are commonplace throughout Russia.

Western businessmen who control the global markets in jewels and precious metals have aided Russian organized crime in their ruthless exploitation of the riches of the Urals. In the oil and gas sector, crime groups have "gained considerable clout . . . by supplying short-term business loans to oil companies and providing access to corrupted government officials who can lobby for favorable legislation, or influence business deals."[25] Their mutually beneficial commerce has facilitated large-scale international fraud and has enabled Urals-based criminal groups to gain footholds in Hungary, Belgium, the Netherlands, Cyprus, and the United Arab Emirates.

Not surprisingly, one of the major activities of economic organized crime in the Urals is legalizing incomes and profits that are earned criminally, (i.e., money laundering). This is done through a variety of mechanisms: buying foreign currency, shipping money abroad to offshore tax havens, creating fictitious companies, buying shares of privatized enterprises, purchasing real estate, and creating charitable foundations. Transnational operations—those that cross national borders—require avoiding or corrupting customs controls. This extra step becomes unnecessary when the laundering is done through investment in the local and regional economies. The latter has the added advantage of facilitating control of some of the most profitable business enterprises in the region. Instead of a simple currency exchange, lucrative growth investments can be made.

Among the important factors that have permitted or encouraged the infiltration of organized crime into the Urals economy are gaps and deficiencies in the law, which is still a mix of old (Soviet) and new provisions, and the lack of effective cooperation among the various law enforcement and regulatory bodies charged with policing the economy. Some of these bodies are newly created and have unclear missions, and almost all such bodies are badly underfunded. In addition, international cooperation is also very hit or miss. Some of the offshore tax havens, for example, refuse to cooperate at all with Russian law enforcement. The relatively facile manner in which Russian organized crime groups have taken advantage of technological advances for criminal purposes, versus the relatively slow and inadequate response of law enforcement to this exploitation, suggests that the criminals are going to stay ahead of law enforcement for at least the foreseeable future.

Organized crime and corruption: Infiltration of the legal and political systems

Experts such as Yakov Glinsky, Senior Researcher at the Institute of Sociology of the Russian Academy of Sciences in St. Petersburg, estimate that between 30 and 60 percent of the income of Russian organized crime is spent on bribery and various forms of political lobbying. To uphold and protect their interests with governmental agencies in both the executive and legislative branches, criminal groups carry out this lobbying in the form of receptions, dinners, trips, and outright cash for reelection. We assume that roughly the same proportionate use of illegal largesse is practiced by the criminal organizations in the Urals. Corruption is a necessary practice for the continued activities of any organized criminal group. What is unique in this situation is the degree to which criminal groups have infiltrated the political process. The Uralmash and central groups in particular have succeeded in electing political candidates favorably disposed towards them, in opposing other candidates, and even in electing their own members to office. This trend towards merging individual political parties and movements with criminal organizations is driven both by the desire of organized crime to influence the political and economic processes and by the needs of these political entities for financial support in amounts that only organized crime can supply.

Investigations and court cases in the Urals region have revealed that corruption, official abuses of power, and representation of the interests of criminal organizations are systemic. These abuses are not idiosyncratic to particular persons who happen to be in power at a particular time; they are endemic to the system of power. They are present at all levels of government, but especially at the regional level. Those agencies responsible for regulating foreign economic matters and for licensing are most vulnerable to corruption.

Because of the latent nature of this corruption, it is difficult to estimate its magnitude or to say much about trends. In 1997, the Sverdlovsk Regional Internal Affairs Department investigated 308 crimes involving corruption. Through the first 6 months of 1998, this number had increased to 199. The main targets for bribes were the police, customs officials, and tax inspectors. For example, the regional prosecutor investigated the case of the director of police in Kamensk-Uralsk, who was regularly receiving payoffs from the head of a criminal organization. In return for his money, the police director covered up or expunged crimes committed by the members of that organization and alerted them to possible investigations. This scenario has been repeated in many police jurisdictions.

The merging of economic organized crime and corruption has had a number of deleterious effects: a warped redistribution of property and capital, a merging of the top leadership of the three most powerful criminal organizations in the region with governmental authorities, and the resultant formation of a powerful criminal lobby that influences important economic and political decisions.

The institutions of government have lost the confidence of the people of the Urals, just as they have lost the confidence of people in the rest of the country. Unfulfilled expectations of what "democracy" would bring, failed reforms, high unemployment, unpaid wages, and the loss of social benefits have all contributed to this loss of confidence and to a growing cynicism. The vacuum of power and government service has been filled in many areas by criminal organizations that have moved to take on some of these governmental functions, providing funds for the repair of schools and hospitals, sponsoring sports events and activities, and setting up charities. As a result, they gain the support and assistance of the people in neutralizing the efforts of law enforcement.

In the Urals industrial center of Nizhni Tagil, the former soccer player "Konstantin" exemplifies this trend. Law enforcement authorities estimate that his criminal organization controls about 60 percent of the criminal market in the area and that it has affiliates in Moscow as well. Despite this, Konstantin is regarded in the Yekaterinburg area as a "Russian Robin Hood." It is not hard to see why. In the overcrowded detention facility in Yekaterinburg, where two remands had died because of the intolerable conditions, Konstantin's criminal group responded by delivering lifesaving medicines, supplies, and foodstuffs. It is estimated that the organization takes about 30 percent of the income of local businesses in extortion payments, but in return provides protection against other criminals and racketeers, guarantees the collection of debts, assists in dealings with the bureaucracy, and lends money at rates much more favorable than those of the banks. As evidence of his community support, when Konstantin was arrested on a racketeering charge, a large group of disabled persons, retirees, and members of the local soccer team sent a letter of protest to the authorities, emphasizing his good works and demanding his release.

Because of the corruption and ineptitude of government, those segments of the society that one would normally expect to oppose organized crime—public organizations, political movements, and the population at large—instead support it. Ironically, organized crime provides stability and fuels the economic engine. This stability and economic stimulation, however, come at a very dear price in the long run.

International threats

The organized crime threat to Russia's national security is metastasizing into a global threat.[26] The criminal organizations that dominate organized crime in the Urals have begun to make their presence known in many other countries as well, operating both on their own and in cooperation with foreign groups. The latter cooperation often comes in the form of joint money-laundering ventures. According to information compiled by regional law enforcement authorities, criminals from the Urals region have been responsible for a number of violent crimes (mainly killings for hire) in Central and Western Europe, Israel, Canada, and the United States. But the economic impact of their criminal activity is what is, perhaps, more distinctive about them.

The Uralmash and blues criminal networks in particular are suspected of involvement in illicit trafficking in such dangerous products as weapons and nuclear materials. Various kinds of hazardous materials have been moved across the porous borders of the Caucasus and Central Asia with the active assistance of criminal groups from those areas. It is a matter of considerable concern to Russian leaders that the smuggling of otherwise legal raw materials deprives Russia of export income and undercuts the world market value of these materials.

THE THREAT OF RUSSIAN ORGANIZED CRIME TO THE UNITED STATES

Russian organized crime, or what has been generically referred to (inappropriately in our view) as the Russian Mafia[a] in the United States, is an umbrella characterization that captures a variety of crime groups and criminal activities. In some instances, the crimes and forms of Russian criminal organizations in the United States differ from those of Russian organized crime elsewhere in the world, including in Russia itself. This is explainable in part by differing external environments and criminal opportunities. In the United States, the label "Russian" actually refers to a variety of Eurasian crime groups. These include Armenians, Ukrainians, Lithuanians, and persons from the Caucasus region of the former Soviet Union (e.g., Chechens, Dagestanis, Georgians). It is estimated that some 12 to 15 loosely categorized criminal groups that have international ties to Russia or other former Soviet republics are currently operating in the United States. These groups, which we will also conveniently label Russian organized crime, together have some 500 to 600 members.

The threat and use of violence is a defining characteristic of Russian organized crime in the United States. Violence is used to gain and maintain control of criminal markets, and retributive violence is used within and between criminal groups. The common use of violence is not surprising, since extortion and protection rackets are such a staple of Russian criminal activity. Contract murders, kidnapings, and business arson have all been employed by Russian organized crime. Arson is used against businesses that refuse to pay extortion money. An example of this violence is reflected in the 1999 convictions of six members of what is referred to as the Gufield-Kutsenko Brigade in New York on Federal racketeering charges involving terrorizing business owners to extort money.

The most defining characteristic of Russian organized crime in the United States is the nature of its criminal activity. With the principal exceptions of extortion and money laundering, Russians have had little or no involvement in some of the more traditional types of organized crime, such as drug trafficking, gambling, and loan sharking. Instead, these varied criminal groups are extensively engaged in a broad array of frauds and scams, including health care fraud, insurance scams, stock frauds, antiquities swindles, forgery and fuel tax evasion schemes. Recently, for example, Russians have become the main purveyors of credit-card fraud in the United States.

Russian organized crime is adept at changing criminal activities and diversifying into new criminal markets. Financial markets and banks, for example, have become new targets of criminal opportunity. In a recent case in point (*United States* v. *Alexander Lushtak*), it was alleged that the defendant carried out a multimillion-dollar investment fraud scheme and the subsequent laundering of nearly $2 million of the proceeds of that scheme by depositing the moneys in an account at the Bank of New York. In *United States* v. *Dominick Dionisio, et al.*, two persons alleged to be associated with La Cosa Nostra and an alleged member of the "Bor" Russian organized crime group were charged with operating a multimillion-dollar investment fraud and laundering the proceeds of the scheme.

Legitimate businesses such as the movie business and textile industry have become targets of criminals from the former Soviet Union, and they are often used for money laundering. A major 1999 money laundering case is illustrative of this recent Russian organized crime activity. That case also involved the Bank of New York (BONY).

In 1999, four individuals and two companies were indicted by the United States in connection with the laundering of more than $7 billion (some estimates range up to $10 billion). Two of those indicted subsequently pled guilty. This case exemplifies a number of the most threatening characteristics of Russian organized crime. First, the moneys laundered apparently represented a mix of criminal proceeds and money being hidden to avoid regulation by the Russian government. This means that Russian organized crime is using institutions such as BONY to launder criminal money, but also to assist Russian businesses and individuals in moving their assets out of Russia so as to evade Russian law enforcement and tax officials. Further, the BONY case illustrates diversification and, even more importantly, a blend of legal and illegal activities that increases the difficulty for U.S. law enforcement in combating money laundering by Russian organized crime. Finally, Russian organized crime clearly has the capacity to tap professional know-how in its financial schemes. As this case and the stock fraud cases demonstrate, some of those associated with Russian organized crime work primarily in the legitimate sectors of the economy. This blend is suggestive of the Urals situation, with the long-term implication that the deeper Russian organized crime penetrates the legitimate economy, the more difficult it will be to dislodge it.

a. See Finckenauer, James O., and Elin J. Waring, *Russian Mafia in America,* Boston, MA: Northeastern University Press, 1998.

The regional department for combating organized crime in the Urals estimates that the theft and export of strategic and precious metals, especially aluminum and copper, is a major source of income for the region's criminal organizations. This highly profitable illicit business is aided and abetted by a tangled web of intermediaries, including foreign firms. Those officials charged with managing the metals aid the thefts, and foreign delivery is made possible by the payment of bribes for the necessary export licenses. The stolen raw materials are sold abroad through well-organized networks, and the moneys received in payment are deposited into accounts held in foreign banks by "shell" companies that exist only on paper.

The arsenals, military units, and defense facilities based in the region are the sources of weapons dealt in arms trafficking. Criminal organizations exploit the weakened military discipline, poor morale, and corruption of military command staff to obtain weapons through both theft and purchase. These arms are then sold abroad via the thriving black market in arms and defense equipment. The regional authorities report that the items purchased range from ammunition and small arms to short- and medium-range missiles and that the countries of the Middle East are a particularly lucrative market for these sales.

Money laundering in Russia is facilitated by weak frontier, customs, and financial controls and the pervasive corruptibility of officials. Profits from arms and drug trafficking and from prostitution, for example, are transferred abroad through banks and other financial institutions. This is usually done by means of fraudulent commercial contracts. In these money-laundering schemes, the Urals criminal organizations are second to none—and that includes the Moscow-based criminal groups. Examples of their handiwork are found in various countries. In Belgium, they have founded a large company for trading in rare and nonferrous metals. They run trading companies in Germany, act as intermediaries between Ural Airlines and Western businessmen, and control individual traders operating in the United Arab Emirates and Greece. They also import criminal capital to be laundered through investment and the banking sector in Yekaterinburg. According to law enforcement sources, one Yekaterinburg-based bank is jointly owned by a local criminal group and members of the Italian-American and Sicilian Mafia organizations.

THE FUTURE OF ORGANIZED CRIME IN THE URALS

What is generally true throughout Russia is especially so in the Urals. As businesses arose or spun off from the old command economy in topsy-turvy fashion, they quickly exceeded the state's ability to regulate and protect them. Since many of those who became engaged in the new businesses already had criminal roots, and the businesses themselves were enmeshed in old black-market and shadow-economy practices, it was not a great leap to the resulting general criminal contamination of its economy that Russia currently suffers. As a consequence of this criminalization, it is impossible to envision today any new commercial activities appearing that will not be under the control of organized crime.

The shape of organized crime in the Urals seems to have formed around two factions into which the elite of the traditional criminal world (the blues) has split. Some of those who up to now have made their careers in crime appear to be moving away from criminal activity and instead are trying to emulate their white-collar brethren. Professional criminals from the old-style criminal underworld who have proven themselves particularly adept at running gambling businesses or at trading drugs or weapons undergo "retraining" or "retooling" to shift over to the more high-powered white-collar crime world. They invest and launder their illegally gotten gains and attempt to assimilate into business and government, apparently viewing such a move as both less risky and more lucrative. Their objective appears to be to maximize their profits, but to do so in ways that are safer than continuing their criminal activity. Thus they are active in real estate, banking, and foreign trade.

Others from the world of career criminals, however, continue to do what they have always done—running rackets, controlling prostitution, dealing in stolen automobiles, and so on. Unlike their colleagues who are making the transition, the latter criminals must continue to worry about their competition in the criminal world, as well as about law enforcement. The gangs and organized criminal groups specializing in violence will undoubtedly continue their criminal exploits, but it is unlikely that they will rival the power and influence of such economic criminal networks as Uralmash.

The nature of organized crime in the Urals has also changed. Economic influence is becoming more important than physical influence. The leaders of the economic organized crime networks do not wield absolute power like "godfathers." Resolution of disagreements and conflicts occur less and less through resort to violence. Instead, mutual economic self-interest seems to dictate these resolutions.

The greatest threat to the West, and to the United States in particular, arises from the expansion of Urals-based criminal activities abroad. The most enterprising of the criminal networks in the Urals are rapidly transforming themselves into transnational criminal organizations. They take their substantial capital and look for opportunities to launder their money and pursue various kinds of business and criminal activity on the global scene.

As the transnational groups accumulate money, power, and influence, government agencies charged with combating them are actually declining in capacity and effectiveness. Neither the federal nor the regional governments possess the resources to counter the burgeoning problem of organized crime. What is more, at all levels of government the political will necessary to tackle the problem seems to be distinctly lacking. As a result, we anticipate that organized crime networks will only become stronger and more powerful in the near future. And because of the deep penetration of the legitimate sectors of the economy, dislodging and suppressing these networks will only be accomplished by means of a costly and lengthy effort, in which the United States can anticipate having to play a major role.

Notes

1. Cockburn, Patrick, "Gang Shoots Dead Businessman Who Confronted Mafia," *Independent Newspapers* (U.K.), July 11, 2000.

2. Gurov, A.I., *Red Mafia*, Moscow: Samotsvet Publishing House, 1995; "A Study of Organized Crime: Russian-American Dialog, The Collection of Articles," Conference report, Moscow State University, Moscow, 1997; Voronin, Y.A., *Criminology*, St. Petersburg: Academy of the Ministry of Internal Affairs, 1998.

3. For example, O'Kane, J.M., *The Crooked Ladder*, New Brunswick, NJ: Transaction Publishers, 1992.

4. According to this law, vory were forbidden from working at legitimate jobs, paying taxes, fighting in the military, and cooperating with law enforcement. Vory had to give up their families to devote themselves to a life of crime. In addition to fighting to uphold the rigid code of rejection of and resistance to the law-abiding world, vory had to contribute to a communal criminal fund called an "obshchak."

5. Gurov, A.I., *Professional Criminality: Past and Present*, Moscow: Judicial Literature, 1990: 207; Luneev, V.V., *The Essence of Organized Crime: The Russian-American Dialog*, Moscow: Moscow State University, 1997: 34.

6. Handelman, Stephen, *Comrade Criminal*, New Haven, CT: Yale University Press, 1995: 56.

7. See Simis, K.M., *USSR: The Corrupt Society*, trans., Jacqueline Edwards and Mitchell Schneider, New York: Simon and Schuster, 1982; and Vaksberg, A., *The Soviet Mafia*, New York: St. Martin's Press, 1991.

8. See Voronin, Y.A., *Criminology* (see note 2).

9. Ibid.

10. Ibid.

11. Ibid.

12. Ibid.

13. Ibid.

14. See *The Commentary of the Criminal Code of Russia*, Moscow: The Institute of State and Law of the Russian Academy of Sciences, 1996.

15. See *Organized Crime*, no. 3 (1996).

16. The research methods employed in this case study reflect the complex and unique difficulties in conducting empirical studies of organized crime. Organized crime is by nature a hidden phenomenon. Penetrating it not only is very difficult, but can be dangerous as well. Law enforcement penetrates organized crime for investigative purposes by using surveillance, wiretapping, eavesdropping, informants, and undercover investigators. These primary methods for collecting information are not, however, tools generally available to the researcher. As a result, researchers must depend to a considerable extent on secondary methods and materials; namely, studying law enforcement reports and interviewing agents and investigators. Both were done in this case study.

   In addition, researchers can take advantage of the investigative work done by journalists. Although journalism is not governed by the same rules for testing the reliability and validity of information as is scientific research, much valuable information can be gleaned from the media. Local newspaper coverage was also used heavily in this case study of organized crime in the Urals. In this case study, because of the pervasiveness of corruption, and because of the desire of powerful individuals to keep much of this material from being publicized, both law enforcement and media sources had to be handled with extreme caution.

17. A number of persons are named here as being involved in criminal activity. Some names are proper names, others are only nicknames, and some are only first or last names. These have been taken from police reports that were made available or from media (mostly newspaper) accounts and are thus as they were recorded in those sources. The leaders involved here were the brothers Grigory and Konstantin Tsyganov.

18. The brightest representatives of the criminal leadership in the region in the late 1980s were such thieves-in-law as Khorkov, Chinar, and Cherepanov, and such gang leaders as Trifon and Ovchina. One particularly distinctive figure among this group was Avarenok, the so-called "ideologist of the blues," and a traditionalist in the criminal world.

19. The key figures in this central group were Oleg Vagin, Mikhail Kuchin, Ivan Kazarian, Sergey Malofeev, and Sergey Dolgushin.

20. Oleg Vagin, a leader of the central group of Uralmash, actively cooperated with various leaders of criminal organizations based in Moscow. The latter included Leonid Bilunov, who was head of the Lyuberetskaya criminal group, and Vladimir Tolmachev, who was a major Moscow banker.

21. This team was under the leadership of Sergey Kurdyumov. The first victim of the Kurdyumov team was Oleg Vagin, the leader of the central group that was affiliated with the Uralmash network. Vagin was killed by machine gun fire in downtown Yekaterinburg on October 26, 1992. Nikolai Shirokov, who headed another affiliated criminal group that specialized in bootlegging, gas stations, and a taxi business in Yekaterinburg, was murdered in Budapest in 1993, along with three of his bodyguards. In November 1996, one of the assassins (Sergey Terentiev) involved in these crimes was arrested at Sheremetyevo airport in Moscow, and by 1997, 16 others had also been arrested and charged.

22. To counter the Kurdyumov assassination team, the central criminal group set up its own team for "elimination," headed by Georgy Arkhipov. The Arkhipov team blew up an Il–76 plane on an airfield in Budapest, assassinated Konstantin Doronin (vice president of the Urals trade house), and made an attempt on the life of Konstantin Tsyganov of Uralmash. When police arrested Arkhipov in Tallinn, Latvia, in 1995 and liquidated the team, they found a huge cache of weapons, including antitank rockets, grenades, explosives, and ammunition. They also found that in addition to Yekaterinburg, Arkhipov had apartments in Anapa, a small city in the south of Russia, and in Hungary and Latvia as well.

23. In the period 1992–98, the following persons were murdered by professional killers: A. Tarlanov (a leader of white-collar organized crime); V. Ternyak (leader of a criminal group and president of the European-Asian Company); S. Malofeev (leader of the central group and president of the Pyramid holding center); S. Dolgushin (criminal leader and president of the business club); V. Kasintsev (director of the Union of Afghanistan Veterans); G. Tsyganov (founder of the Uralmash criminal group); and V. Benyaminov (a leader of the Syrian community in Yekaterinburg and co-owner of the Elisaveta shop that was allegedly used for money laundering).

24. Chinar, Avarenok, Khorkov, and others.

25. U.S. Government Interagency Working Group, "International Crime Threat Assessment," December 2000: 68.

26. Williams, P., ed., *Russian Organized Crime: The New Threat*, special issue, 2 (2/3) (1996).

About the National Institute of Justice

NIJ is the research and development agency of the U.S. Department of Justice and is the only Federal agency solely dedicated to researching crime control and justice issues. NIJ provides objective, independent, nonpartisan, evidence-based knowledge and tools to meet the challenges of crime and justice, particularly at the State and local levels. NIJ's principal authorities are derived from the Omnibus Crime Control and Safe Streets Act of 1968, as amended (42 U.S.C. §§ 3721–3722).

NIJ's Mission

In partnership with others, NIJ's mission is to prevent and reduce crime, improve law enforcement and the administration of justice, and promote public safety. By applying the disciplines of the social and physical sciences, NIJ—

* **Researches** the nature and impact of crime and delinquency.

* **Develops** applied technologies, standards, and tools for criminal justice practitioners.

* **Evaluates** existing programs and responses to crime.

* **Tests** innovative concepts and program models in the field.

* **Assists** policymakers, program partners, and justice agencies.

* **Disseminates** knowledge to many audiences.

NIJ's Strategic Direction and Program Areas

NIJ is committed to five challenges as part of its strategic plan: 1) **rethinking justice** and the processes that create just communities; 2) **understanding the nexus** between social conditions and crime; 3) **breaking the cycle** of crime by testing research-based interventions; 4) **creating the tools** and technologies that meet the needs of practitioners; and 5) **expanding horizons** through interdisciplinary and international perspectives. In addressing these strategic challenges, the Institute is involved in the following program areas: crime control and prevention, drugs and crime, justice systems and offender behavior, violence and victimization, communications and information technologies, critical incident response, investigative and forensic sciences (including DNA), less-than-lethal technologies, officer protection, education and training technologies, testing and standards, technology assistance to law enforcement and corrections agencies, field testing of promising programs, and international crime control. NIJ communicates its findings through conferences and print and electronic media.

NIJ's Structure

The NIJ Director is appointed by the President and confirmed by the Senate. The NIJ Director establishes the Institute's objectives, guided by the priorities of the Office of Justice Programs, the U.S. Department of Justice, and the needs of the field. NIJ actively solicits the views of criminal justice and other professionals and researchers to inform its search for the knowledge and tools to guide policy and practice.

NIJ has three operating units. The Office of Research and Evaluation manages social science research and evaluation and crime mapping research. The Office of Science and Technology manages technology research and development, standards development, and technology assistance to State and local law enforcement and corrections agencies. The Office of Development and Communications manages field tests of model programs, international research, and knowledge dissemination programs. NIJ is a component of the Office of Justice Programs, which also includes the Bureau of Justice Assistance, the Bureau of Justice Statistics, the Office of Juvenile Justice and Delinquency Prevention, and the Office for Victims of Crime.

To find out more about the National Institute of Justice, please contact:

National Criminal Justice Reference Service
P.O. Box 6000
Rockville, MD 20849–6000
800–851–3420
e-mail: *askncjrs@ncjrs.org*

To obtain an electronic version of this document, access the NIJ Web site
(*http://www.ojp.usdoj.gov/nij*).

If you have questions, call or e-mail NCJRS.

U.S. Department of Justice
Office of Justice Programs
National Institute of Justice

Washington, DC 20531

www.ingramcontent.com/pod-product-compliance
Lightning Source LLC
Chambersburg PA
CBHW080620180526
45168CB00007B/2995